Canadian Trees

Canadian Cataloguing in Publication Data

Mastin, Colleayn, O. (Colleayn Olive)
    Canadian Trees

Nature Canada Series; 3

    ISBN 1-895910-02-1 (bound). - ISBN
    1-89510-05-6 (pbk.)
    1. Trees—Canada—Juvenile literature.
    I. Sovak, Jan, 1953- II. Title.   III. Series.
    QK201..M388 1994 j.582.160971 C93-091871-1

PUBLISHED BY~

GRASSHOPPER BOOKS
106 - WADDINGTON DRIVE
KAMLOOPS, BRITISH COLUMBIA
CANADA V2E 1M2

A portion of the sales
of this book will be
donated to the
Canadian Nature Federation

This book is dedicated to January, Tiffany, Lindsay, Jody and Adrianne-Monique.

Acknowledgement

The author wishes to thank the following individuals for their contributions to this book ~ Francoise Sveistrup, Dr. Hubert Bunce, Dean Purych, Dan Holden, Barry Kenoras, Ken Uyeda, Wendy Nankivell, Kathryn Burkell, Dennis Johnson

DESIGN & PRODUCTION BY ~ BLACKBIRD DESIGN, CALGARY, ALBERTA
PRINTED IN CANADA BY ~ FRIESEN PRINTERS LTD., ALTONA, MANITOBA

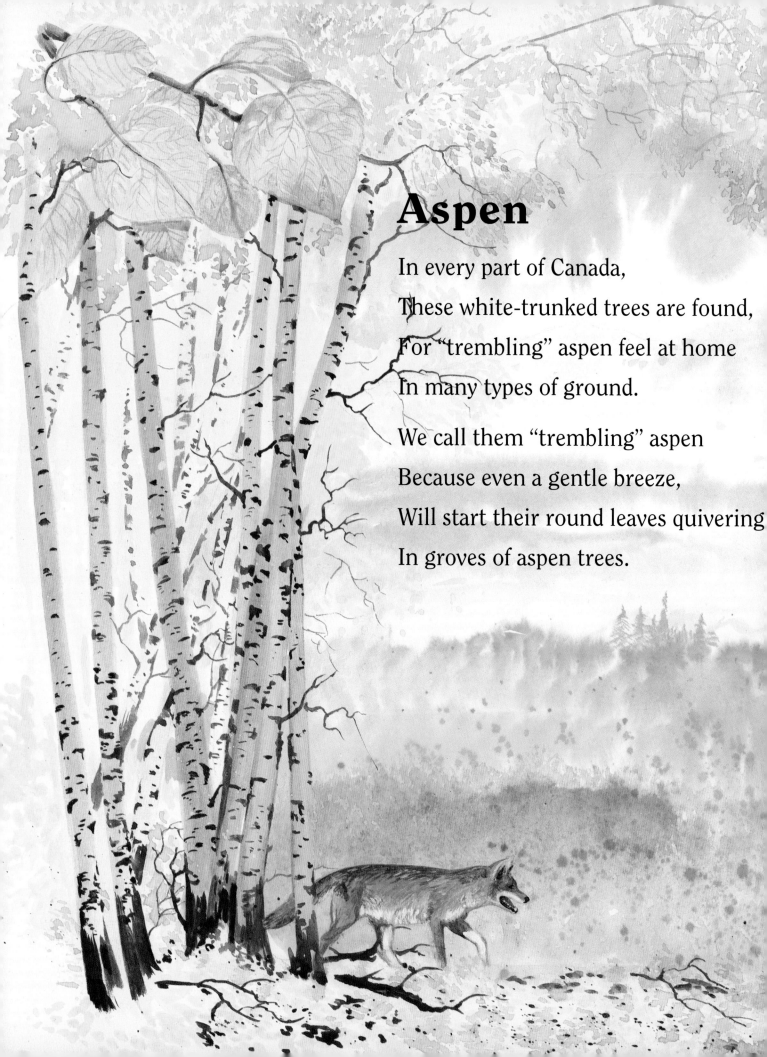

Aspen

In every part of Canada,
These white-trunked trees are found,
For "trembling" aspen feel at home
In many types of ground.

We call them "trembling" aspen
Because even a gentle breeze,
Will start their round leaves quivering
In groves of aspen trees.

If you ever get lost in the woods, an aspen tree could help by letting you know in what direction you are facing. The chalky white material that is found on its bark is always thickest on the south side of the tree.

Aspen is used to make paper, toilet tissue, matches, plywood, boxes and snowboards. This tree is a tasty food for the beaver. Native people once ate the inner bark, raw or roasted. They also called it the "noisy leaf tree" because of the sound it makes when the wind blows.

Fir

Firs are graceful,tall, strong trees,
With narrow pointed crowns;
These trees make jobs for people
In dozens of lumbering towns.

The largest tree that grows
in Canada is the Douglas fir.

You can tell the difference
between fir and spruce needles
by rolling them between your
finger and thumb. Spruce needles
will roll, while fir needles are flat.

The tallest firs seem to touch the sky,
As they sway in a wind or a breeze;
Much smaller firs we set on stands
And call them Christmas trees.

and will not roll.

Lichen grows on the branches of the Douglas fir.
This is a very important food for the caribou in the forest.
When the wind blows the lichen falls off the branches
and the caribou eat them for winter food.

Fir is used for building houses because the
wood is very strong.

Cedar

Some Native Indian people used to make their canoes out of birch bark, though the West Coast Indians still carve magnificent canoes and totem poles from the mighty cedar. Years ago, they used the tree's stringy bark to weave cloth for clothing and blankets.

Longhouses, where the people of some communities lived, were also made from cedar logs.

Many forest birds use this tree for their nests. The spotted owl builds its nest in holes in the trunk and the majestic bald eagle builds its nest on the very top.

Cedar wood does not rot quickly, so it is very good for fence posts, cedar shakes, roofs and for the siding of houses.

A yellow cedar seed once planted, can take up to two thousand years to become a giant tree. A red cedar takes about one thousand years to become a gigantic tree.

The cedar tree has stringy bark,
Its dark green leaves lie flat;
This scented wood makes trunks and chests,
To store your coat and hat.

And from its soft and straight-grained wood,
We make shingles, shakes and siding,
And all those lines of cedar fence
You can see when you go riding.

Birch

The lovely birch is tall and straight

With white and papery bark;

It grows wild in many a forest,

And tame in many a park.

Along our mighty rivers and streams

Indians paddled their birch bark canoes;

Now birch is used for popsicle sticks,

So you don't drop the stuff on your shoes.

The wood from birch trees is used to make wonderful things like toys, school desks, bookcases, paper, boxes and skateboards. When you go skating down the street, remember, that's a tree beneath your feet. Native people used this tree to make baskets and canoes.

The birch tree normally grows in open areas. If you peel the bark from a dead birch, it can be used as a good starter for campfires. The birch is the provincial tree of Saskatchewan.

Hemlock

You can tell this tree's a hemlock
By the top branch of its crown,
For its slender, whip-like "leader"
Gracefully droops down.

Native Indians used hemlock bark
To make bread they loved to munch;
And from hemlock pulp comes cellophane
That we use to wrap our lunch.

The tiny seeds that fall from the cones of the hemlock have wings that can carry them through the air to find a spot where they can sprout and grow. These seeds are food for birds and mice, while rabbits and beavers eat the tender little seedlings. Deer will eat the leaves and twigs from older trees.

Because the roots of hemlock trees do not grow deep into the ground, sometimes snow and wind will topple them. Those that do survive, can live for four or five hundred years.

Hemlock is a very important tree in the lumber industry. It is used to build houses, and to make cardboard boxes, telephone poles, broom handles, and paper.

Sitka spruce is the tallest, though not the largest, of our native trees. In the early days of flying, many airplanes were made out of Sitka spruce.

Many centuries ago, when the explorer Jacques Cartier and his men were suffering from the disease called scurvy, the Indians gave them tea made from spruce needles. This helped them to get well.

Native people of the west coast used the roots and branches of the spruce trees to weave hats and to make baskets. The gum from the tree is now used to make candy, chewing gum, and medicine.

Spruce is a very important tree for the lumber industry. It is used for building houses, and for making plywood, crates, cabinets, and paper.

Spruce

This very tall and straight trunked tree,

Is an evergreen called the spruce;

It grows all over Canada

And of it we make great use.

It's especially good for paper,

So next time you have a cold,

And reach for a piece of tissue,

That's part of a spruce you hold.

Forests

Imagine a world without forests;

How awful it would be,

To travel across our country

And never see a tree.

Our forests give us many things,

Wild birds and some bears live there,

Without forests, we would not have,

That wonderful stuff called air.

Forests are called "The Lungs of the Earth". The leaves of trees give off the oxygen which is important to all creatures who breathe. This is one of the main reasons we must see that the forests of the world are maintained.

Trees provide shade for animals and humans. They also act as windbreaks to shelter crops and homes, hold the soil in place with their roots, and provide beauty for all to see.

The forest is home for wild animals and birds. People, such as birdwatchers, hikers, swimmers, painters, photographers, berry pickers, and fishermen all share the forest with the animals. The forest also provides the raw materials for products such as paper, lumber, and medicines.

Tamarack

The northern swamps of Canada
Are home to the tamarack;
From its wood we make the ties
That carry a railroad track.

Since the tamarack's a conifer,
It should stay green all year,
But its needles turn yellow in fall,
And get scattered far and near.

The tamarack tree is special because it is a cone-bearing evergreen and should keep its needles all year but it does not.

It drops its needles in the fall like the leaves of a deciduous tree. Then, in the spring, the tamarack needles grow back again, just the same as the leaves that grow back on deciduous trees.

Tamarack is used to make pulp for books, newspapers, railway ties, and for building construction lumber. Tannin, a substance used for tanning leather, is taken from the bark of the tamarack.

Pine

In the east, white pine is famous,
Ponderosa is a western pine;
The evergreen needles on both trees
Are long and very fine.

Pine trees will grow in places
Where the soil is not that good,
But in spite of this, most pine trees,
Give us soft and useful wood.

The Ponderosa pine is sometimes called the "Jig-Saw Tree". The bark of older trees flakes off into chunks that look like the pieces of a jig-saw puzzle.

There are over thirty kinds of pines growing in Canada. One pine tree is named the lodgepole pine. This tree grows tall, straight, and slim. Because of this, native people used this tree for building tepees and lodges. They also used the inner bark, which they boiled and mashed to make bread. The sweet orange sap is also good to eat.

If you look around your house, you will probably see pine wood that has been used to make doors, window frames, wooden matches, boxes, crates, and the cabinets in your kitchen. The early settlers in Canada used pine for making furniture. The white pine is the official tree of Ontario.

Maple

The red maple leaf on Canada's flag
Is known the whole world through;
This tree gives excellent furniture wood,
And delicious syrup, too.

To make this tree our emblem,
We really were quite clever,
Now all Canadians hope we keep
Our maple trees forever.

Not all maple trees produce the sap that can be turned into maple syrup or maple sugar. The best sugar maples grow in eastern Canada. It takes about thirty litres of maple sap to make one litre of this wonderful, sweet-tasting syrup for our pancakes.

This tree is very important for wildlife. Birds build their nests in these beautiful trees and also feed on the seeds. Deer eat the young twigs and buds. Porcupine eat the bark, but if they strip it totally around the trunk, they can kill this handsome tree. The maple leaf was chosen for the Canadian flag in 1965.

Fruit Trees

All of our trees are useful
For the good things that they bring,
But fruit trees are quite special,
For they blossom in the spring.

Some bear sweet fruit in autumn,
That we and the birds can share;
So let's give thanks for the apple and plum,
The cherry, the peach and the pear.

The fruit trees that we have in the orchards were brought here by the first settlers that came to homestead in Canada.

Just as they brought cows, sheep, goats, pigs and other animals that were not native to Canada, pioneers also brought grafts of the fruit trees from their old country homes so that they could grow them in orchards here. They blossom in the spring and bear fruit in the summer and fall.

Some animals, such as deer, horses, cows and birds, enjoy eating the fruits that grow in the orchard. The leaves and bark of some fruit trees can be used to make medicine.

Oak

The oak is called the "King of Trees",
Its growth is long and slow;
You'd wonder how such mighty oaks
From tiny acorns grow.

There are many types of oak trees
To name them might get boring,
But one thing should be noted—
These trees make great oak flooring.

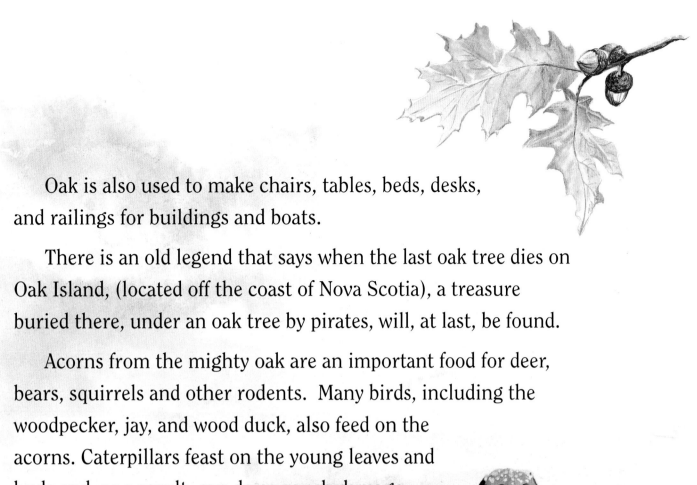

Oak is also used to make chairs, tables, beds, desks, and railings for buildings and boats.

There is an old legend that says when the last oak tree dies on Oak Island, (located off the coast of Nova Scotia), a treasure buried there, under an oak tree by pirates, will, at last, be found.

Acorns from the mighty oak are an important food for deer, bears, squirrels and other rodents. Many birds, including the woodpecker, jay, and wood duck, also feed on the acorns. Caterpillars feast on the young leaves and buds and, as a result, can do so much damage that sometimes the tree dies.

Elm

Elm trees grow mostly in the east,
Their wood is very tough;
They live for years and grow up tall,
Their bark is grey and rough.

We plant elm trees along our streets
To give us summer shade,
And out of elm, long years ago,
Our hockey sticks were made.

In the early days, hockey sticks were made out of elm. These trees became scarce after they were attacked by a disease, so hockey sticks were then made from other hardwoods, such as birch, ash, hickory and maple. Today most hockey sticks are made out of a combination of all these woods, or from synthetics.

Elm is used to make barrels, boxes, piano frames, boat frames, and caskets.

The seeds and buds of this medium sized tree are food for songbirds, game birds and animals such as the deer and rabbit. Beavers and muskrats feed on the bark.

Tulip Tree

There are flowers on this poplar,

So it's called the tulip tree;

It grows across Ontario;

And some places in B.C.

This lovely tree grows tall and straight,

Its leaves are green and square;

They turn yellow when the autumn wind

Sends them dancing through the air.

Can you imagine a tree with the name of a flower?

Most trees have leaves that are rounded or pointed, but the tulip tree has leaves that are almost square. Its leaves are very distinctive and have the shape of a tulip. This is why this tree received its name.

This tall, beautiful tree also known as a yellow pine is classed as a hardwood tree. This is because it has broad leaves, rather than the kind of needles that are found on pine or fir. Its wood is soft and easy to work with. It is used to make furniture, toys, and some musical instruments.

Yew

Compared with other evergreens,
The yew tree's kind of short;
Its sharp flat leaves are poisonous,
I really must report.

It's mostly out on rough, wet land
That scraggly yew trees grow;
Old Robin Hood used yew tree wood,
To make himself a bow.

The seeds of the yew tree are surrounded by a small, red cap. This cap is not poisonous, though the seeds and leaves are. Birds know this, so they eat the cap, then scatter the seeds.

Scientists have discovered that the bark from the yew tree contains a drug called taxol. It is being used as a treatment for cancer. The taxol is in the bark, but if the bark is taken from the tree it will die. Foresters now grow plantations of yews, to make sure that we will always have a supply of these useful trees.

In the olden days, yew trees were planted in graveyards. The graveyards were fenced and therefore cattle could not get in to eat these trees. As a result, soldiers could be sure that a source of yew wood was available to make their bows.

Canadian Trees Quiz
Questions

1. When the explorer Jacques Cartier and his men were suffering from a disease called scurvy, the Indians gave them tea and this helped them get well. What was the tea made from?

2. Which tree is also called the "Jig-Saw Tree" and why?

3. How can you tell the difference between fir and spruce needles? How does each feel?

4. Which tree is called "The King of Trees"?

5. Why is cedar used for fence posts and siding for houses?

6. What is aspen used for?

7. What is special about the maple tree?

Answers

1. Spruce needles.

2. Ponderosa pine - because its bark breaks away in scales that look like the pieces of a jig-saw puzzle.

3. Roll them between finger and thumb. Spruce needles will roll and are quite prickly. Fir needles are flat, will not roll and are soft to the touch.

4. The oak is call the "King of Trees".

5. Cedar wood does not rot quickly.

6. The maple leaf is on the Canadian flag. Maple syrup is made from the "sugar" maple tree.